BIGGEST SCANDALS IN SPORTS

IN SPORTS

BY TYLER MASON

THE WILD WORLD OF
SPORTS

SportsZone

An Imprint of Abdo Publishing
abdopublishing.com

abdopublishing.com

Published by Abdo Publishing, a division of ABDO, PO Box 398166, Minneapolis, Minnesota 55439.
Copyright © 2018 by Abdo Consulting Group, Inc. International copyrights reserved in all countries.
No part of this book may be reproduced in any form without written permission from the publisher.
SportsZone™ is a trademark and logo of Abdo Publishing.

Printed in the United States of America, North Mankato, Minnesota
102017
012018

Cover Photos: Amy Sancetta/AP Images, foreground; Laurent Rebours/AP Images, background
Interior Photos: Everett Collection/Newscom, 5, 6; AP Images, 7, 8, 11, 13, 14, 15, 16–17, 32; Matty
Zimmerman/AP Images, 10; Marty Lederhandler/AP Images, 18; John Martell/AP Images, 19; David
Breslauer/AP Images, 20–21; David Durochik/AP Images, 23; Al Behrman/AP Images, 24; Gregory Bull/
AP Images, 25; Merline Summers/AP Images, 27; Andreas Altwein/picture-alliance/dpa/AP Images, 28;
Denis Paquin/AP Images, 29; Beth A. Keiser/AP Images, 30–31; Bill Clark/CQ Roll Call /AP Images, 33;
Rusty Kennedy/AP Images, 35; Haraz N. Ghanbari/AP Images, 36; David J. Phillip/AP Images, 39; Peter
Dejong/AP Images, 41; Alexander Gordeyev/Shutterstock Images, 42; Stringer/Photoshot/Newscom, 43;
Shutterstock Images, 45

Editor: Meg Gaertner
Series Designer: Craig Hinton

Publisher's Cataloging-in-Publication Data

Names: Mason, Tyler, author.
Title: Biggest scandals in sports / by Tyler Mason.
Description: Minneapolis, Minnesota : Abdo Publishing, 2018. | Series: The wild world of sports | Includes
    online resources and index.
Identifiers: LCCN 2017946929 | ISBN 9781532113628 (lib.bdg.) | ISBN 9781532152504 (ebook)
Subjects: LCSH: Sports--United States--History--Juvenile literature. | Sports--Miscellanea--Juvenile
    literature.
Classification: DDC 796--dc23
LC record available at https://lccn.loc.gov/2017946929

TABLE OF
CONTENTS

CHAPTER 1

BLACK SHEEP
OF BASEBALL

Baseball player Joe Jackson once wore only socks for a minor league game because his shoes weren't broken in. A reporter at the game gave him the nickname "Shoeless" Joe. Jackson didn't like the nickname, but it stuck. Jackson played 13 seasons in the major leagues. He had a lifetime batting average of .356, which is the third-best of any player in Major League Baseball (MLB) history. Many people believe Jackson should be in the Baseball Hall of Fame. But he might never be, because he was banned from baseball for life.

Jackson played for the Chicago White Sox in 1919. The White Sox were the American League champions and were heavily favored to win the World Series. When they lost to the Cincinnati Reds, many in the baseball world thought there was something suspicious about the outcome.

"Shoeless" Joe Jackson was one of several White Sox players implicated in the Black Sox Scandal.

Two years before the scandal, Jackson, *center*, and the White Sox beat the New York Giants in the 1917 World Series.

Eight Chicago players were accused of taking money from gamblers to intentionally lose the World Series. Three Chicago players admitted they had cheated. Jackson said he took the money but did not change the way he played. His .375 Series batting average was the highest of the regular players on either team. Though none of the eight players were arrested, all were banned from baseball for life in 1921. The controversy became known as the Black Sox Scandal.

KENESAW MOUNTAIN LANDIS

In response to the cheating that was taking place, Major League Baseball (MLB) owners named Judge Kenesaw Mountain Landis the game's first commissioner in 1920. One of his first jobs as commissioner was to place a lifetime ban on the eight players involved in the Black Sox Scandal. Landis eventually banned 10 more players from other teams for cheating and gambling.

Kenesaw Mountain Landis was the MLB commissioner until his death in 1944.

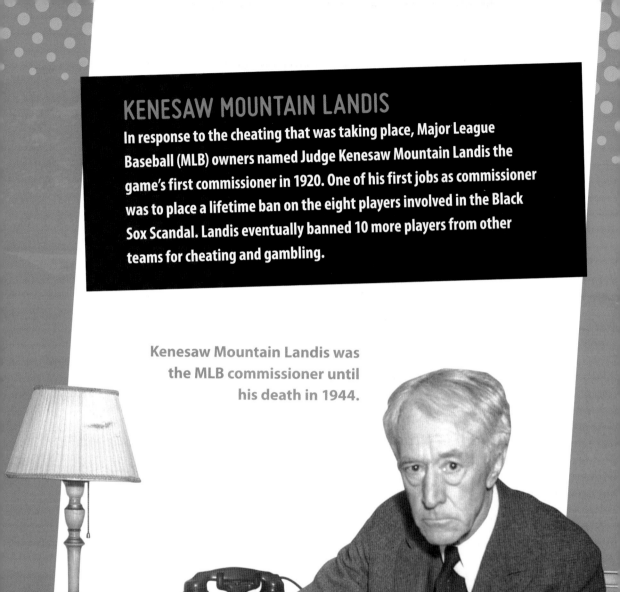

8

CHAPTER 2

SHAVING SHAME

ew York City was the center of the college basketball world in 1950, mainly because of the City College of New York (CCNY) Beavers. Many players on the team were the children of immigrants, making the team as diverse as the city it played in.

By the end of the 1949–50 season, the Beavers ranked seventh in the country and had made it to two national championships. At the National Invitation Tournament, the Beavers trounced defending champion San Francisco and favored Kentucky to win the title. The Beavers also won the National Collegiate Athletic Association (NCAA) tournament, beating Bradley by three points.

Less than a year later, these victories were forever tarnished by the arrests of seven of the team's stars for point shaving. The players admitted to accepting money in exchange for manipulating the score—winning or losing games by a prearranged number of points

Al Roth, *center*, was one of the CCNY players charged with fixing games.

to benefit gamblers betting on the games. CCNY players shaved points in six games, including three they deliberately lost during the 1950–51 season.

Fans of CCNY were not the only ones crushed by the arrests. The scandal that rocked New York City implicated more than 30 players from seven colleges around the country, including Bradley

CCNY coach Nat Holman, *right,* accepts the NCAA championship trophy in 1950.

CCNY players Irwin Dambrot, *left*, and Herb Cohen are booked in a New York police station in 1951.

and Kentucky. Collectively, these players were accused of fixing more than 80 games between 1947 and 1951.

In the end, the seven CCNY players turned over the money they had accepted. Five of the players received suspended sentences, one joined the Army to avoid being sent to a workhouse, and one went to prison for six months. All seven were banned from ever playing in the National Basketball Association (NBA).

THREE SECONDS
TO GLORY

By 1972 the United States men's basketball team had won the Olympic gold medal at seven consecutive Olympic Games. The most recent victories, in 1964 and 1968, were won under coach Henry Iba's leadership. Iba and the team appeared to be a lock to win again in the 1972 Olympic Games in Munich, West Germany. But no one could have predicted what would take place in the gold-medal game against the Soviet Union.

Doug Collins made two free throws with three seconds to play, giving the United States a 50–49 lead. It would take a miracle for the Soviet team to win. The Soviets threw the ball inbounds from under their own basket and dribbled to half-court before the buzzer sounded. Their coaches argued they had called a timeout between Collins's free throws. The referees, who had not acknowledged the

Center Dwight Jones (9) and Team USA faced the Soviet Union in the basketball finals at the 1972 Olympic Games.

Soviet center Alexander Belov scores the winning basket in the controversial final seconds of the game.

timeout, put three seconds back on the clock. The Soviets inbounded the ball again and threw up a long shot that hit the rim as the buzzer sounded. Thinking they had won the gold medal, the Americans began celebrating.

But the Soviet Union got one more chance. The referees said the clock had not yet been reset when gameplay resumed, so they gave the Soviets another inbounds play. The third time was the charm. Center Alexander Belov of the Soviet Union caught a long pass under the US basket. The American defenders could not knock the ball away. Belov scored easily just before the clock hit zero, and the Soviets defeated the United States 51–50.

The Americans filed a complaint about the clock issue. However, the International Basketball Federation ruled that the Soviet Union had won. The US players refused their silver medals and remained bitter about the outcome for years.

The Soviets took home the gold and Cuba won the bronze, but the silver-medal US team skipped the award ceremony.

AN UNBELIEVABLE
TIME

For eight days, Rosie Ruiz was the winner of the 1980 Boston Marathon. On April 21, Ruiz finished the famous race in 2 hours, 31 minutes, and 56 seconds. Her time was the third fastest ever by a woman in a marathon. It beat her time in the 1979 New York City Marathon by 25 minutes.

There was just one problem. Ruiz did not run the entire 26.2 miles of the race. People noticed Ruiz was not very sweaty after the race. Spectators said they did not see her running at the beginning of the marathon. Her improved marathon time made other runners suspicious, and her lack of training drew questions from fellow competitors.

Rosie Ruiz receives the laurel wreath after being announced winner of the women's division of the 1980 Boston Marathon.

A race official monitors footage that will disqualify Ruiz from the 1979 New York City Marathon.

Thousands of photos and extensive video were shot of the race, but Ruiz appeared only in those showing the last half-mile. Members of the crowd said they saw Ruiz join the marathon near the end of the race. Ruiz never admitted that she cheated, but her title was taken away on April 29. Canadian runner Jacqueline Gareau was declared the winner.

A RUIZ REPEAT

Rosie Ruiz cheated in the Boston Marathon in 1980. A husband and wife tried the same thing 17 years later. John and Suzanne Murphy each took first place in the senior categories in 1997. The Murphys were later disqualified for not running the entire course and banned from the Boston Marathon for life.

It was later discovered that Ruiz had also cheated in the New York City Marathon in 1979, where she finished in 24th place. Witnesses saw Ruiz riding the subway during the marathon. She was eventually disqualified from that race, too.

Three weeks after the Boston Marathon, Jacqueline Gareau, *right*, is declared winner due to Ruiz's disqualification.

THE DEATH PENALTY

In the 1980s, Southern Methodist University (SMU) had a student body of only 6,000 students. But the small school in Dallas, Texas, made a big impression in college football. The Mustangs went undefeated in 1982 and won the Cotton Bowl, thanks in part to star running back Eric Dickerson. Talented players were committing to play for SMU instead of more traditional football powers in the region, such as Texas and Oklahoma. Dickerson himself chose to play at SMU after originally committing to Texas A&M.

The NCAA found out why. SMU boosters were paying some of the players. The punishment SMU received has been referred to as the death penalty. The NCAA forced the Mustangs to cancel their 1987 season. The school also did not play during the 1988 season. Missing out on two seasons hurt SMU's program for a long time. Since returning in 1989, the Mustangs had only four seasons with winning records through 2016.

Eric Dickerson, *left*, takes a handoff during the Cotton Bowl, which SMU won to finish the season undefeated on January 1, 1983.

CHARLIE HUSTLE

Pete Rose was given the nickname "Charlie Hustle" because he hustled whenever he played baseball. Rose won almost every baseball award possible. He was Rookie of the Year in 1963 with the Cincinnati Reds. He was voted the National League's Most Valuable Player (MVP) in 1973. He also played in six World Series and was named Series MVP when the Reds beat the Boston Red Sox in 1975.

Rose won three batting titles and two Gold Glove awards in 24 seasons. He played in more games and has more hits than any other player in MLB history. He also became manager of the Cincinnati Reds. Despite his achievements, Rose is not in the Baseball Hall of Fame.

Rose's final year as manager was in 1989, the same year he was banned from baseball for life. Rose was accused of betting on baseball games. MLB rules specifically state that those connected with the game will be permanently banned if they are caught gambling on games in which they are involved.

With all his accomplishments, Pete Rose would be a Hall of Fame shoo-in were it not for his gambling.

MLB appointed lawyer John Dowd to lead the investigation. The Dowd Report determined that Rose did indeed bet on baseball games in 1985, 1986, and 1987. Rose was still playing when he began betting on baseball, and he gambled on his own games both as a player and as a manager.

Baseball's all-time hits leader denied the charges for years. Rose finally admitted that he bet on baseball games in 2004 in his book *My Prison Without Bars*. But Rose said he made bets only when he was a manager. He denied betting on games as a player.

John Dowd investigated the gambling allegations against Pete Rose.

The lifetime ban made Rose ineligible for the Baseball Hall of Fame, but he remains popular with his longtime fans.

A report based on one of Rose's notebooks later found that Rose did bet on baseball games as a player in 1986. Rose tried to have his ban lifted in 2015 but was denied. MLB commissioner Rob Manfred declared Rose would remain banned from the game.

RINK RIVALRY

Nancy Kerrigan and Tonya Harding were teammates and rivals on the US national figure skating team. They were very different people, and they had very different skating styles. Harding was a powerful skater who amazed fans with her jumps and spins, while Kerrigan was viewed as graceful. They came from different economic backgrounds as well. Kerrigan wore elegant skating outfits made by fashion designers. Harding sometimes had to make her own outfits.

Their rivalry hit a low point one month before the 1994 Olympic Winter Games. Both skaters were practicing in Detroit, Michigan. A man attacked Kerrigan before her practice on January 6, clubbing her hard on the right knee. Kerrigan didn't know if she would recover in time to skate in the Olympics. She also did not know the man who hit her.

An investigation was launched immediately. The trail led directly to a number of people in Harding's inner circle.

Tonya Harding, *left*, and Nancy Kerrigan pose for the 1994 US Figure Skating Championships, a competition Kerrigan was not able to attend due to injury.

One month after the attack, Harding, *left,* and Kerrigan shared the ice during the 1994 Winter Olympics.

Harding's ex-husband, Jeff Gillooly, arranged the attack. He paid Shane Stant, an acquaintance of Harding's bodyguard, $6,000 to attack Kerrigan. Stant went to jail for 18 months and Gillooly for two years for their headline-making crime.

Though she missed the 1994 US Figure Skating Championships, Kerrigan recovered in time to compete in the Olympics. But the media circus that followed her and Harding to Lillehammer, Norway, wasn't helpful for athletes who needed to concentrate and be mentally focused. Kerrigan skated well, but Ukrainian teenager Oksana Baiul edged her out for the gold medal.

Harding finished in eighth place. Though she never admitted to knowing about the planned attack, Harding was banned for life by US Figure Skating and had to pay a fine of $100,000. She never skated competitively again.

Oksana Baiul, *center,* upset Kerrigan for the gold medal in Lillehammer.

HOME-RUN HYSTERIA

Energized by a historic home-run race, baseball fans were glued to their televisions in 1998. St. Louis Cardinals first baseman Mark McGwire and Chicago Cubs outfielder Sammy Sosa each had a shot at breaking the single-season home-run record. Roger Maris of the New York Yankees hit 61 home runs in 1961. Nobody had come close since.

MLB's television ratings soared because of the home-run battle. Ballparks around the league kept track of McGwire's and Sosa's homers on their scoreboards. Both players broke Maris's record that season. McGwire got there first and ended the season with an astonishing 70 home runs. Sosa finished with 66.

But McGwire's record would eventually become tarnished. He admitted in 2010 to using illegal performance-enhancing drugs for many years, including during his 70-homer season. Sosa never admitted to using drugs, but a report indicated that he had tested positive for steroid use in 2003.

The St. Louis Cardinals' Mark McGwire and the Chicago Cubs' Sammy Sosa were both implicated in MLB's steroid scandal.

The home-run battle of 1998 took place during baseball's so-called "Steroid Era," which dated from the late 1980s to the mid-2000s. During that period many baseball players took performance-enhancing drugs, partly because MLB did not test for steroids until 2003. Before that rule took effect, McGwire's record was shattered by Barry Bonds. The San Francisco Giants outfielder slammed 73 homers in 2001.

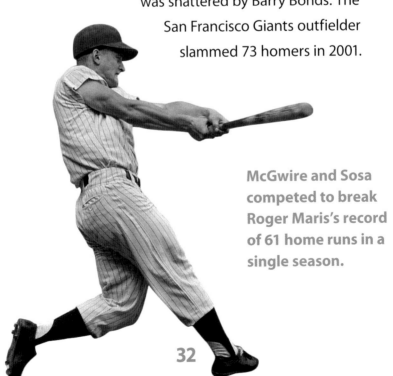

McGwire and Sosa competed to break Roger Maris's record of 61 home runs in a single season.

Former Senator George Mitchell authored a report on the use of steroids in Major League Baseball.

Other famous players took steroids during that time. Alex Rodriguez admitted to it. Rafael Palmeiro failed a drug test in 2005. Bonds also admitted he took steroids but claimed he didn't know what he was taking at the time. Bonds's record is acknowledged by MLB, but he and others caught up in the scandal have been shunned by Baseball Hall of Fame voters.

THE LITTLE GIANT

Danny Almonte dominated in the 2001 Little League World Series. A native of the Dominican Republic, he played with a team from the Bronx, New York. Almonte pitched a perfect game and struck out 16 batters in one of his starts. He faced 72 batters in four games and struck out 62 of them.

Why was Almonte so much better than his opponents? At 5 feet, 9 inches, he was taller than most of the other players. He was also at least two years older than them. Players in the Little League World Series must be 12 years old or younger. Almonte was 14. His birth certificate listed a wrong date of birth. The error was not discovered until after the Little League World Series. Almonte's team lost 8–2 in the US championship game. Almonte went on to a brief professional career after high school.

Danny Almonte throws a pitch during the 2001 Little League World Series.

PLAYING THE ODDS

Two groups paid Tim Donaghy when he was an NBA referee. The NBA paid him his regular salary. He also received money from gamblers.

Donaghy refereed his first NBA game in 1994 and eventually became a mainstay in the league. He worked more than 60 NBA games a season for many years. It wasn't until late in his career that Donaghy started betting on basketball games. Law enforcement first became suspicious of his actions in 2007. The Federal Bureau of Investigation began looking into his activities and found that Donaghy gave information about games to gamblers, something that is illegal for referees to do.

As a referee, Donaghy could influence the game's outcome. He would use secret codes during phone calls with gamblers. Gamblers made a lot of money when Donaghy gave them information about

Tim Donaghy made thousands of dollars by giving gamblers information about the games he refereed.

which team would win. Donaghy was paid $5,000 every time that information was correct.

Donaghy eventually admitted to what he had done and pleaded guilty in court in August 2007. Nearly one year later, he was sentenced to 15 months in prison. Donaghy was released from prison after 13 months. The former referee wrote a book about the scandal. It was to be titled *Blowing the Whistle: The Culture of Fraud in the NBA*. But at the last minute the publisher canceled its plans. Some in Donaghy's corner suggested the NBA had pressured the publisher to scrap the book, a charge the league denied.

BLOWING THE WHISTLE

Nine years after he went to prison, Tim Donaghy was in the headlines for making claims about the 2017 NBA Finals. Donaghy said the NBA wanted the Finals to go to a sixth game, implying that the referees would make calls to alter the game. He had made a similar claim during the 2016 Finals.

TOUR DE FRAUD

In 1995, Lance Armstrong finished in 36th place at his first Tour de France, professional cycling's most famous race. He was 23 years old. A year later he was diagnosed with cancer, which had already spread throughout his body. He went into surgery the day after his diagnosis. Surviving cancer would be miracle enough. But Armstrong went on to win the Tour de France a record seven times.

Only two years after being declared cancer-free, Armstrong began a seven-year winning streak between 1999 and 2005 at the Tour de France. His success inspired many people to start cycling. Millions of people wore yellow Livestrong bracelets, which were sold to raise money for Armstrong's charity and to promote cancer awareness. Armstrong retired from professional cycling in 2011. One year later he was banned from cycling for life.

Whispers about his cheating had dogged Armstrong since he tested positive in a drug test before his 1999 win. A doctor's note

Lance Armstrong carries the US flag after winning his seventh consecutive Tour de France.

Armstrong received much media attention, both for his cycling success and for his doping scandal.

claimed the steroid had come from a skin cream. Investigations in 2002, 2005, and 2010 also fell through, and Armstrong maintained his innocence.

It wasn't until 2012 that the US Anti-Doping Agency charged Armstrong with taking performance-enhancing drugs during his career. His seven Tour de France titles were taken away, and he also had to give back his bronze medal from the 2000 Olympic Games.

During a 2013 interview with Oprah Winfrey, Armstrong finally admitted to taking performance-enhancing drugs for training and recovery. He said he does not regret taking them and later admitted he would probably do it all over again.

Armstrong, *left,* first admitted to doping in an interview with talk-show host Oprah Winfrey.

CHAPTER 12

SOCCER SHOCKER

Law enforcement officers raided a fancy hotel in Switzerland in May 2015 and turned the soccer world on its head. The Fédération Internationale de Football Association (FIFA) is the organization that governs international soccer. Fourteen of its top officials were arrested during the raids in Switzerland. The FIFA members were accused of corruption for allegedly having received more than $150 million in bribes for television contracts.

FIFA president Sepp Blatter resigned not long after the arrests. Though he was not one of the people arrested in Switzerland, he was banned from soccer for eight years. Gianni Infantino replaced Blatter as FIFA president. The scandal hurt soccer's image. FIFA lost millions of dollars in 2016 because sponsors no longer wanted to advertise with the organization. Another FIFA scandal was uncovered in March 2016. FIFA admitted to awarding the rights to host the World Cup based on bribes.

Sepp Blatter stepped down as FIFA president amid allegations of bribery and corruption.

GLOSSARY

batting average
A baseball player's number of hits divided by the number of at-bats.

betting
Gambling money on the outcome of a sporting event.

booster
A person who donates time and financial resources to promote an institution's athletic programs.

bribe
Money given to someone, usually illegally, to persuade or influence a decision.

commissioner
The chief executive of a sports league.

hustle
To work quickly and with great energy.

marathon
A race 26.2 miles in distance.

point shaving
When a player or players on a team purposely alter the score of a game to make sure their team wins or loses by a prearranged number of points.

steroids
Drugs taken to improve an athlete's performance or ability to recover from training.

ONLINE RESOURCES

To learn more about the biggest scandals in sports, visit **abdobooklinks.com**. These links are routinely monitored and updated to provide the most current information available.

MORE INFORMATION

BOOKS

The Editors of Sports Illustrated Kids. *Big Book of WHO Basketball: The 101 Stars Every Fan Needs to Know.* New York: Time Inc. Books, 2015.

Herman, Gail. *What Are the Summer Olympics?* New York: Grosset and Dunlap, 2016.

Panchyk, Richard. *Baseball History for Kids: America at Bat from 1900 to Today with 19 Activities.* Chicago, IL: Chicago Review Press, 2016.

INDEX

ABOUT THE AUTHOR

Tyler Mason studied journalism at the University of Wisconsin–Madison. He has covered professional and college sports in Minneapolis and St. Paul, Minnesota, since 2009. He currently lives in Hudson, Wisconsin, with his wife.